STA

STA

Katie's Cabbage

Katie's Cabbage

Katie Stagliano

with Michelle H. Martin

Illustrated by Karen Heid

Foreword by Patricia Moore-Pastides

THE UNIVERSITY OF SOUTH CAROLINA PRESS

*Publication is made possible in part by the generous support of
Bonnie Plants and First Fruits Marketing of Washington.*

This book is dedicated to my friends at
Bonnie Plants, whose Third Grade Cabbage Program
started my dream, and to my family, who, through
their support, enabled me to help fight hunger,
one vegetable garden at a time!

Foreword

Katie Stagliano is a bright star in this world. She is a tenacious young woman with a great, hope-filled heart, a true empathy for others, and a keen understanding of how to get things done. With her wonderfully supportive family, Katie has taken on one of the most pervasive and desperate needs of our time: fighting hunger.

Katie was an impressive ten-year-old when we first met at Pinewood Preparatory School in Summerville, South Carolina, in 2009. Because I had recently begun an organic vegetable garden at the University of South Carolina, Katie was invited to show me around the vegetable garden at Pinewood Prep.

As we strolled the large fall garden complete with pumpkin-headed scarecrows, Katie told me the story that you are about to read—the story that began all of the amazing work Katie has done since. She impressed me then as a sweet girl, passionate about her goals, and it was easy to see she was achieving them and then some!

Katie's now-famous cabbage started her on a journey that has become a mission in her young life. She not only cultivates a garden, donates the harvest, and helps cook meals for the hungry, but she also started a nonprofit organization to help support other like-minded young gardeners across the United States, served on a taskforce of the United Nations, and became the youngest recipient of President Bill Clinton's Global Citizen Award for Leadership in Civil Society.

Katie's story shows us all how much good one person can do in the world, and how much good we all can do when working together with family and friends. Katie continues to envision a world without hunger, and she inspires and challenges us to do whatever we can to bring that dream to life.

Patricia Moore-Pastides, M.P.H.

First Lady, University of South Carolina
Columbia, South Carolina

I sat at my desk, eagerly awaiting the bell announcing the end of the school day for my third-grade class.

RING! We all jumped out of our seats and ran toward the door. "Remember to grab a cabbage seedling on your way out! And remember to use plenty of T.L.C.," said Mrs. Andrews as we started to leave the classroom.

Dozens of cabbage seedlings nestled in black plastic trays sat near the door. I spotted a small one in the corner with three tiny green leaves: the perfect seedling. I gently picked it up and headed out to my mom and John Michael, my four-year-old brother, ready to go home.

As my mom's car pulled into our driveway, I grabbed my backpack and hopped out of the car with today's math lesson fresh in my mind. John Michael followed, carrying the seedling, which he placed on the kitchen counter. I sat down at the table with a bag of pretzels, ready to tackle my homework. The first math problem mentioned gardening, which reminded me of my seedling.

"John Michael, let's go plant my cabbage seedling," I said. Grabbing the seedling off the counter, I ran into the garage to collect two shovels and some gardening gloves.

I searched the backyard for a good home for my seedling. Under the palm tree was too shady. By the fence got too much sun. The beds with the gardenias and roses in them were too crowded.

Then I spotted just the right place. It was perfect!

My brother and I dug a hole. I pulled the tender seedling from the pot.

"Wait!" I cried. "We almost forgot to use T.L.C.."

"What's T.L.C.?" asked John Michael, confused.

"We have to treat the seedling with Tender Loving Care."

John Michael nodded, and we carefully dug until the hole was twice the size of the cabbage plant. We then eased the plant into the earth and filled in the rest of the hole with dirt. My seedling had found a new home. I high-fived John Michael, and we went back inside.

Mom handed me a watering can and said, "Don't forget to water, sweetie."

Every day after school, I checked on my cabbage, pulled out weeds that would steal its nutrients, and watered the plant to help it grow.

And grow it did!

I was amazed at how fast. It was soon as big as a soccer ball and getting bigger by the day.

Whenever my friends came over to play, they checked out just how big my cabbage had grown. Soon the whole neighborhood began to notice.

"Hey Katie, what are you feeding that thing? It's almost the size of your brother," said Ms. Rose from next door.

Dr. Sheppard agreed. "Katie, that is one beautiful cabbage."

But Mr. Gable from down the street had some bad news: "Katie, some deer ate the shrubs in my yard yesterday. If I were you, I'd keep an eye out."

Would deer eat my cabbage if there was nothing to protect it? I called my grandfather, Opa, who is an excellent carpenter. He would know just how to keep my cabbage safe.

"Opa, Mr. Gable saw deer in his yard, and I'm worried they'll eat my cabbage."

He promised to help. "Tomorrow after school, I'll come over, and we'll build a cabbage cage."

"Deal," I answered.

True to his word, Opa came over the next day with his tools, and we built the cage. We put wooden posts in the ground, hammered nails into the boards in the shape of a large box, and wrapped it in chicken wire. Hours later, when we were finished, the cage looked, well, "interesting," but I didn't care about looks because I knew it would protect my cabbage from becoming a deer's snack.

One night as my family sat down to dinner, my dad asked us if we knew how lucky we were to be able to sit down to a good meal every night. "Some families go to bed hungry because they don't have enough to eat."

"Really?" I asked. I'd never thought about this before.

"Yes, sometimes people do not have enough money to buy food. All over the world, some kids and adults go to bed hungry," my dad explained.

I sat there quietly thinking about this: if kids just like me all over the world go to bed with empty bellies then maybe I could help.

"I can give my cabbage to families who don't have enough to eat!" It made me so happy to think of all the good my cabbage could do. I asked Mom if she would help me find that special home where it could do the most good.

She smiled and said, "Of course, sweetie!"

And she did. The next day Mom called around and found Fields to Families, an organization that gets fresh vegetables from farmers to soup kitchens to feed the hungry.

"Hello. This may sound a little odd, but my daughter, Katie, grew a large cabbage as a school project, and she would like to donate it to help feed families in need. Can you help us with this?"

Miss Jackie, the woman on the other end of the phone said, "I have the perfect home for Katie's cabbage."

After school, I asked Mom if she had found a home for my cabbage.

"Yes, your cabbage will go to Tricounty Family Ministries to feed families in need."

This was great news, but I had so many questions: "Where is Tricounty?" "How many people does it feed?" "When can we go there to help?"

Just a week later, my cabbage was the perfect size to harvest—gigantic!

Together, my family and I went into the backyard, tools in hand. John Michael had a yardstick to measure my cabbage, and my dad had a saw to cut it from its stalk and roots. I had a wheelbarrow to transport my cabbage to our car, and my mom had her camera to capture this exciting moment.

I thought back to my cabbage as a tiny seedling. Now look how big it had grown with T.L.C.! It was amazing!

John Michael held the yardstick up to the cabbage as Mom took the picture. Then I gave my cabbage a hug just before Dad sawed the giant ball of green leaves from the ground.

John Michael and I tried with all our might to lift the cabbage, but it wouldn't budge. Dad had to help us lug it to the wheelbarrow. When we got it to the driveway, the three of us lifted the cabbage into the back of our SUV, and we all hopped into the car, eager to donate my cabbage.

As we pulled into the Tricounty Family Ministries parking lot, I stared at the long line of people that wrapped from the parking lot to the front door of the small house. The line seemed endless. "All those families, just like mine," I thought.

As we passed the line I heard, "Wow! Look at that amazing cabbage!"

"Is that for us?"

"That sure will be delicious!"

Ms. Sue, the director of Tricounty, walked out, her arms open to greet us. "What a beautiful cabbage, Katie! Come on in! Let me show you the kitchen."

We followed Ms. Sue into the small kitchen, with Dad now carrying the cabbage in his arms. We saw shelves filled with pastries and loaves of bread. Men and women carried large pots and trays of hot food. A young man pushed a cart of chocolate cakes.

In another area, women wearing plastic gloves and hairnets served rice, chicken, salad, and beans with metal spoons and tongs. Other adults passed food and drinks to the waiting guests at windows. Outside, behind the kitchen, were picnic benches packed with people eating their meals.

When Ms. Sue introduced me to the kitchen staff, one of the women suggested we weigh the cabbage. Dad placed the cabbage down on a scale in the storage room. The number blinked a couple of times before stopping.

"Young lady, you've grown yourself a *forty-pound cabbage*. That's quite an accomplishment!" announced the head cook.

"What are you going to make with it?" I asked.

"I think we're going to pair your cabbage with some ham and rice. We'll have ourselves a nice meal for a whole lot of folks."

"That sounds yummy!" I replied, pleased.

Ms. Sue invited us to come back later in the week to help serve my cabbage to the guests. Friday could not come fast enough. When I saw the sign for Tricounty from our car window, I said, "We're here!" John Michael and I unbuckled, eager to work.

Ms. Sue greeted us outside. "I'm so excited you're here! Come in, and we'll get you all ready to serve."

She handed me a large black apron that went down to my knees, plastic gloves, and a large serving spoon. I sat on a wooden stool next to three women who were also serving. The cook set a large metal dish in front of me. When he lifted the lid, steam billowed out, and, when the steam cleared, I saw my cabbage . . . transformed. No longer the giant ball of green leaves that had to be sawed down like a tree, my cabbage was now ready to be served.

One of the women said, "Wow, that sure looks delicious!"

The women scooped rice and ham onto a plate and passed it to me. I added a heaping portion of cabbage. After me, others added salad, a roll, a piece of cake, and a drink, and then the meal was handed off to a little girl about my age. Hundreds of hungry people followed her, including boys and girls of all ages.

Many of the kids stood there, tugging at their parents' shirts or playing rock-paper-scissors to pass the time. Two little kids even started singing. As they got their meals, they smiled and thanked the volunteers and me, then ate together on the porch.

John Michael was helping another volunteer, Doc, pass out the bread and treats over a wooden half-door. Since John Michael was too small to see over the half-door, he handed the bags to Doc to be passed out.

The whole meal lasted about two hours.

After I helped to serve the last person, Ms. Sue came up to me with a big smile. "Katie, thank you for your cabbage today." She gave me a warm hug and added, "And thanks for your help too, John Michael." After many more good-byes, we all piled into the car and headed home.

"Wow," I said. "I never knew how many people go to soup kitchens. It seemed like hundreds of people in line! We have to do more to help."

"What would you like to do?" Mom asked.

"I don't know yet," I sighed. "I want to help people at the soup kitchen get great meals every day. But what can a kid do?" As I wondered about this, an idea started to grow in my imagination, just as that forty-pound cabbage had grown with T.L.C. in our backyard.

"I could start a garden and give away everything I grow to a soup kitchen! The spot in our backyard where I grew my cabbage. . . . that's where I'll grow even more vegetables for the hungry."

"What a great idea," Mom and Dad agreed. "Tomorrow, let's get planting!"

The next day we went to the garden supply store. I was so excited about helping to feed all of those people in line at Tricounty.

"Wow, Katie, look at all the tiny plants," John Michael said, amazed.

"There are so many choices. What should we plant?" my dad asked.

"How about peppers and tomatoes and eggplant and basil and cucumbers and squash and okra and collards and. . . ."

"Whoa, slow down, Katie!" My mom laughed. "How about we start with a little less?"

"Okay. Basil, tomatoes, and peppers." I smiled.

We gathered all the plants for the garden and filled the cart completely.

At home, we unloaded the dirt and plants in the backyard. On the very spot where my forty-pound cabbage had grown, John Michael and I laid out the seedlings. Following the instructions on the tiny plant tags, we dug holes and arranged the plants by which ones needed the most sun. Two hours later, we had turned my cabbage's old home into a huge, beautiful, giving garden. I could then only imagine the boxes of healthy, delicious vegetables this would provide for hungry kids and adults. I could hardly wait!

"Wow," John Michael said. "It looks so cool!"

"I agree," Mom said. "Good job, sweetie! This was a wonderful idea."

Three days later, a note arrived in the mail for me.

I was so happy and proud. If one cabbage could feed 275 people, then imagine how many more a whole garden could help.

I ran to my parents to show them Ms. Sue's note. I grinned, knowing this was just the beginning!

About the Author

The story you have just read is true. Katie Stagliano is a real girl living an extraordinary life in service to others. Realizing how one cabbage from a third-grade class project had helped fight hunger in her community, Katie began to pursue a dream of growing additional gardens and dedicating the harvests to feeding families in need. After planting a garden in her own backyard, Katie also wrote a letter to the headmaster of her school, Pinewood Preparatory School, asking if she could expand her gardening vision there to help even more people. Dr. Glyn Cowlishaw responded by giving Katie, then a fourth grader, a plot of land on campus the length of a football field. Then Katie found a mentor in Lisa Turocy, a recent graduate of the South Carolina Clemson University Cooperative Extension Master Gardener Program. Each season, Katie and Lisa have worked side-by-side in the garden, utilizing lessons learned. A wonderful friendship took root between them and continues to this day.

In 2009, Katie officially founded Katie's Krops, her not-for-profit kid-based organization. The mission of Katie's Krops is to start and maintain vegetable gardens of all sizes, to donate the harvests to help feed the hungry, and to assist and inspire others to do the same. Word began to spread of the big efforts of the young girl in South Carolina and of her dream to end hunger one vegetable garden at a time. To expand her local efforts and support the work of other young gardeners across the country, Katie began to offer grants for children ages 9 to 16 to start vegetable gardens where the harvests could be donated locally. Children of all ages from coast to coast submitted their applications because they wanted to help people in their own communities. As a result of this continued response, Katie's Krops now supports more than eighty gardens in twenty-nine states.

All gardens are youth-focused so that children get to play a vital part in ending hunger. Katie's Krops gardens provide a sustainable solution to hunger while teaching kids about agriculture, the environment, nutrition, responsibility, and compassion. The gardens produce thousands of pounds of healthy, fresh produce every year.

In September 2012, Katie became the youngest recipient ever of the Clinton Global Citizen Award for Leadership in Civil Society, given in recognition of her humanitarian efforts. In addition to her work through Katie's Krops, she served for three years on the Youth Advisory Board for the Alliance for a Healthier Generation, and she was a 2012 Global Teen Leader for the Three Dot Dash, a global initiative that supports teen leaders from around the world who are actively working on projects that promote a more peaceful society by addressing basic human needs.

To learn more about Katie and Katie's Krops, please visit www.KatiesKrops.com.

Additional Resources

Bonnie Plant's third-grade cabbage program: http://bonniecabbageprogram.com

Sodexo Foundation: www.sodexofoundation.org/hunger_us

Kids Gardening, a resource of the National Gardening Association:
www.kidsgardening.org

Plant a Row for the Hungry, a program of the Garden Writers Association:
www.gardenwriters.org/gwa.php?p=par/index.html

Clemson University Cooperative Extension: www.clemson.edu/extension/hgic/index.html

American Horticulture Society's master gardener program: www.ahs.org/master_gardeners

Young Palmetto Books

Kim Jeffcoat, Series Editor

Published by the University of South Carolina Press
Columbia, South Carolina 29208

www.sc.edu/uscpress

Manufactured in the United States of America

24 23 22 21 20 19 18 17 16 15   10 9 8 7 6 5 4 3 2 1

Library of Congress Cataloging-in-Publication Data
can be found at http://catalog.loc.gov/.

ISBN: 978-1-61117-504-2 (hardbound)
ISBN: 978-1-61117-505-9 (paperback)